DATE DUE

JUN 1 4 1997			
NOV 2 1 1997			
MAR 1 3 1998			
MAY 1 9 1998			
OCT 0 9 1999			
MAY 0 9 2000			

DEMCO

GRIZZLIES

GRIZZLIES

MARY ANN McDONALD

T H E   C H I L D ' S   W O R L D®, INC.

Photo Credits
Joe McDonald: front cover, 2, 6, 10, 13, 15, 19, 20, 23, 24, 26, 29, 30
Duke Conrad: 9, 16

Printed in the United States of America.

Library of Congress Cataloging-in-Publication Data
McDonald, Mary Ann
Grizzly Bears/Mary Ann McDonald
p.   cm.
Includes index.
Summary: Describes the behavior, habitat, and physical characteristics of the most feared bear in North America, the grizzly.
ISBN 1-56766-213-7 (hard cover : library binding)
1. Grizzly bear--Juvenile literature. [1. Grizzly bear.
2. Bears.]
I. Title.
QL737.C38M357   1996
599.74'446--dc20   95-45350
                          CIP
                          AC

TABLE OF CONTENTS

You stop and listen very closely. From over the next hill you hear singing—the bear went over the mountain, to see what he could see. Your teacher always told you to walk quietly when in the woods. But the singing gets louder. You see a sign on the path where you are walking. It says:

You are in Grizzly Bear Country.
For your own safety, please make
noise while hiking this trail.

Now you understand why people are singing!

A grizzly bear stands in a field.

North America has three kinds, or **species**, of bears. There are *black bears*, *polar bears*, and *grizzly bears*. Polar bears are the largest. Black bears are the most common. But grizzly bears are the most feared animal in North America. The grizzly's scientific name is *ursus arctos horribilis*. It means "horrible arctic bear"!

Grizzly bears are the most feared animal in North America.

Grizzly bears once lived throughout the western United States. Famous explorers, including Lewis and Clark, ran into grizzly bears. Trappers and miners had many problems with bears. Settlers killed almost all of the grizzlies in the western states.

Today, grizzlies are **endangered**, or in danger of dying out, throughout the West. They live only in Idaho, Montana, and Wyoming. Many grizzlies, though, still live farther north, in Canada and Alaska. The grizzlies that live along the Alaskan coast are called *brown bears*. These bears are also found in many parts of Asia and eastern Europe.

Grizzly bears live in the high mountain country.

WHAT DO GRIZZLIES LOOK LIKE?

Grizzly bears vary in color. Some are light tan or blond. Others are almost black. Most grizzlies are brown. The hairs on the bear's back and shoulders have white on their tips. This makes the bears look frosted, or "grizzly."

Grizzlies have a huge hump across their shoulders. They also have a very broad face and a stubby nose. Grizzlies look different from black bears. Black bears don't have a hump. Their faces are smaller, with a pointed nose.

A grizzly bear has a broad face, stubby nose, and a hump on its back.

Grizzly bears can stand on their hind legs. An adult grizzly can stand at least ten feet high. It could dunk a basketball without even jumping! Native Americans called the grizzly "the bear that walks like a man."

A grizzly bear can stand on its hind legs.

WHAT DO GRIZZLIES EAT?

Grizzly bears are **omnivores**, which means that they eat both plants and animals. They eat berries, fruits, grasses, roots, and mushrooms. They also eat ground squirrels, fish, caribou, elk, and deer. Grizzlies even eat dead animals. They find the dead animals by tracking down the smell.

Grizzly bears love to eat salmon.

ARE GRIZZLIES IN DANGER?

Male bears, called **boars**, will kill young bears. A mother grizzly will fight any bear that threatens her babies. There can be lots of fights. Older bears also fight young bears. Sometimes even adult bears get killed.

A grizzly bear cub calls to its mother.

HOW DO GRIZZLIES LIVE THROUGH THE WINTER?

Grizzlies live in areas where the winter is very cold. How do they survive?

During the fall, bears eat a huge amount of food in a short period of time. They eat eighty to ninety pounds of food a day! They are building up layers of fat on their bodies. This fat can be ten inches thick. The fat helps the bears survive during the winter.

Grizzly bears live where the winter is very cold and snowy.

The bears sleep, or **hibernate**, for the whole winter. They sometimes wake up during this long sleep, but they never go outside. Instead, they stay in their cozy little homes, called **dens**. Bears hibernate in caves, big hollow logs, or holes they dig under brush piles or big rocks.

The bears do not eat or drink anything while they are hibernating. Instead, they live off their thick layers of fat.

A grizzly bear comes out of its den in springtime.

HOW ARE BABY GRIZZLIES BORN?

A female grizzly, or **sow**, gives birth while she is hibernating. She has between one and four babies. They are called **cubs**. The cubs are blind and almost hairless at birth. They open their eyes when they are ten days old. During hibernation, the cubs drink only their mother's milk. The mother doesn't drink or eat anything during this time.

A female grizzly watches her cub, who was born during hibernation.

Cubs stay with their mothers for two to three years. They play, climb trees, and learn what to eat. Cubs start eating solid food after they leave the den. They grow very fast. A cub might weigh only a pound and a half at birth. It might weigh 1,500 pounds only eight years later!

Grizzly bear cubs grow very fast.

HOW DANGEROUS ARE GRIZZLIES?

A sow with cubs is one of the most dangerous animals in the wild. Several people have been killed when they surprised a mother and her cubs. A sow grizzly will attack without warning. And grizzlies can run 35 miles per hour for a short distance! People cannot run that fast.

Visitors in bear country make noises when hiking or horseback riding. They sing, talk loudly, and wear "bear bells." The key to safety is to make lots of noise. If a bear hears someone coming, it will hide.

A grizzly bear mother watches over her cub.

WHERE CAN YOU SEE GRIZZLIES?

You can see grizzly bears in Yellowstone and Glacier National Parks. They are fun to watch. But you should always follow park rules. Stay one hundred yards away from any bear. That is as long as a football field! Stay in your car if the bear is close. Do not feed the bears or any other wild animals. And make plenty of noise while hiking.

Enjoying nature and wild animals can be fun and safe. Just remember, be nature smart!

A grizzly bear cub plays in a field.

GLOSSARY

boar (BOR)
A male bear.

cub (KUB)
A baby bear.

den (DEN)
A hollow spot where a bear lives during the winter. Bears make these homes in caves, hollow logs, or holes they dig under brush or rocks.

endangered (en-DANE-jerd)
In danger of dying out.

hibernate (HY-bur-nate)
A very deep sleep. Bears hibernate during the winter.

omnivore (AHM-ni-vor)
An animal that eats both plants and animals. Grizzlies eat many different kinds of food.

sow (SOW)
A female bear.

species (SPEE-sheez)
A separate kind of an animal. Grizzlies are one kind, or species, of bear.

INDEX